THE
INSPIRATION

SHE

WAS LOOKING
FOR

SHE : THE INSPIRATION THAT SHE IS LOOKING FOR

For information contact :
Tonyrogerscc@gmail.com

Book interior design by JK PUBLISHING HOUSE, LLC
ISBN : 9780578848334

First Edition : January 2021

10 9 8 7 6 5 4 3 2 1

THE
INSPIRATION
SHE
WAS LOOKING
FOR

CAPTAIN OF HER DOMAIN

Don't let anyone break your spirit or shatter your dreams. U will come across many obstacles, & face unspeakable challenges. But U won't let them get the best of U, bcuz U are a Soldier that can fight, a Survivor that is resilient & a Queen that deserves her crown. Every day U have a chance to be a better U, so why not start today~TR

SHE'S AN INSPIRATION

She is a force to be reckoned with. She is blessed with the ability of caring for others unconditionally. She has a voice that know one can quiet down. Her mind is complexed bcuz it's always on the move. Her heart is open for the things that she is passionate about. She's a role model to those that believe in her. Sometimes she forgets how much of a blessing she truly is to the world. She is a great person, she has a beautiful soul, & her positive vibes keeps her forever humble. ~TR

DO U APPROVE

Touch her heart to make her feel like the only one. Touch her mind to reassure that your mental connection is in sync with hers. Touch her emotions to let her know you're about sharing feelings. Touch her soul to help her feel that the passion is real. Touch her funny bone to make her smile & brighten up the room. Last but not least, touch her hand to let her know she's not walking this journey alone. ~TR

THE FOOT IS DOWN

Sometimes she just needs her space from the world to recharge her batteries. Battling stress or/and anxiety can be really exhausting & overwhelming on her mind, body, & soul. She's an over thinker that does get burnt out once in a while. She's done dealing with rude, toxic, selfish, narcissistic, & negative ppl that try to bring her down. She will no longer put up with it. This is her year, her happiness, her moment, her time to shine & she will live her life just way she wants to. If U don't like it? U can kiss her azz (sorry I meant) kick rocks. ~TR

T.E.R.R.I.F.I.C

(T) is for Truthful, bcuz she’s tired of being lied to. (E) is for Emotions, bcuz she's full of them. (R) is for Regulator, bcuz she will put your azzin check if needed. (R) is for Romance, bcuz she hopelessly believes in it.(I) is for Intelligent, bcuz her life experiences has taught her well. (F) is for, Forgettable, something she will never be. (I) is for Incredible, something shewill always remain. (C) is for Congratulations, U were the motivation for the inspiring words~TR

HER MIND IS ALWAYS MOVING

She has so many thoughts that run thru her head, U really never know what she's thinking. She has secrets that she will never share, bcuz they are to personal. Externally she doesn't show the scars that she has going on internally. Life has put her thru her battles that made her a great fighter. Her Spirit is strong, her heart is hopeful & her mind is driven She is a mountain that will always be admired for her mysterious & natural beauty~TR

JUST TELL HER

She's wondering why she feels like the guilty one. Why do ppl make her feel like somethings wrong with her? She tries to be the best person should could be, & puts herself out there for others. All she wants in return is honest words spoken to her, even if those words hurt. She's a big girl that can take the good with the bad. Handling rejection will be a tough one, but she will be alright. Just communicate with her, & give her a chance to make her own decision in what she wants to do. Her personality is more down to earth than U give her credit for. Wherever U plant that seed she will always grow~TR

REBELLIOUS

She's impossible to hold back, bcuz of her drive & determination. She's a fighter that won't give up, bcuz she chooses to live her life to the fullest. She can't be stopped, she will be heard, & her movement will be felt. She's a boss lady that don't have time for chicken heads &ratchet ppl. U can never predict what her next move might bcuz U can't/won't see it coming. She's a winner who wins often & is always one step ahead of the game. ~TR

SELF TAUGHT

She keeps her head up, and does her best to be the best version of herself. Sometimes she can't believe the BS experiences she has gone thru, & how she even survived to stay mentally focused this long. Growing with each lesson she has come across has made her ready for the next big challenge. Never doubt her ability. Just peep her skills on how she handles things like a boss. Remember when it's all said & done, she will come out on top some way or another. ~ TR

APPRECIATE HER

She is something out of this world when her heart, mind, body, & soul is there for U. When she gives U the best of her, U will see an angel at work & know U are in blessed hands. Her ability to care for others is unconditional, & her positive energy is strong. She will make sure your safe, lift your spirits when your down, & will have your back when U feel like giving up. She's truly a good person that just wants the great ppl in her life to be happy. ~TR.

THE W

She's a good Woman With great Wheel power When needed. She's Wis e beyond belief. She's a Wishful thinker & she's Willing to give U her all or nothing. She's a Wonderful person that believes Winning is more important internally than materially. Even tho she Whines at times, she's no Wimp. She's a caring & nurturing human that holds the World in her heart~TR

HER TIME

She said takes 8 hours to be considered beauty sleep. It takes 30mins or more to get her out the bed after hitting snooze repeatedly. Her time is precious & important, so she tries not to let the wrong ppl, waste her time. She will make time for those who value her, respect her, & believe in what's important to her. She just wants the time she gives U to be appreciated. ~TR

THE QUESTION

How does she do it? We will never know. Once U think U have her all figured out, U don't. She's 2 steps ahead of the game & her past experiences have made her a pro in dealing with nonsense. She's not perfect, but she will school U, teach U, & if U get out of line, she will check U at the door. She's firm, she knows what she wants, & she's a thinker. The few things we do know about her is that she has a big heart for the ppl she cares about. Her passion is strong when she believes in something. The strength that powers her drive comes from within, which makes her an unstoppable force. ~TR

HER VISION IS CLEAR

The blindfold is off. Now she can see what is real & what is BS. Some of the ppl she believed to be in her corner backstabbed her or used her for whatever reason. Her kindness has been overlooked. Her thoughtfulness, unappreciated. Her unconditional love left undiscovered. She found it unacceptable to not be respected for the good woman she is. She treated others the way she wished to be treated. She deserves the greater things in life, bcuz she is so damn tough when times are so damn hard. She is a bigger person on the inside than most ppl will ever be. She will achieve the impossible, & make positive moves to better herself. ~TR

STRAIGHT FORWARD

There comes a moment when she will have to move on, no matter how difficult it may be. She fights so many battles that know one ever gets to see, & like a blanket she will cover up the deepest scars life has given her. Survival is in her DNA, so she will stay strong to never show her weakness. She's from a town called "I don't take BS from nobody", so be very careful when dealing with her & watch what U say. She's harder than a diamond, sharper than a blade, & one hell of a great person if U get to know her. ~TR

ONE DAY @ A TIME

She has 2 choices: Either to let the world beat her down, or let it see the best in her. Each day she prays to herself, hoping that it will be a stress free, no drama day. Even tho she can't predict the way things will turnout, she will still see it thru to the end. Her focus is to Never give up, Never stop believing, & Never stop pushing thru the grime of the day. Once she realizes how powerful she really is or can be, there will be no stopping her. When she reaches that point in her life, she will feel invincible, & that's when U will see how incredible she truly is. ~TR

A STAR IS BORN

When U came into the world, U were beautiful, small, & innocent. As U grew, U were clueless, & unaware of BS. In time U wised up bcuz of what life showed& taught U. The dark times U experienced made U realize how important the light inside of U meant. Today U are phenomenal, strong, intelligent, compassionate, resilient & a star that will also shine in her own special way. ~TR

SHE GOT THIS

U carry the weight of the world on your shoulders, but ppl would never know. U battle with over thinking about things you're going thru, but yet no one can tell. U been internally hurt/crushed but your poker face hides it very well. U define the meaning of a true fighter bcuz U find the strength to stand up everyday. U are inspirational, courageous, & tougher than leather~TR

THE CHAMPION

To meet her is a blessing. To be in her presence makes U feel lucky, & when talking to her U will gain knowledge U didn't see coming your way. When she's in your corner, U best believe she has your back more than U could I magine. She's emotional, empathetic, intelligent, sarcastic, & so much more than meets the eye. Many have tried to defeat her, suppress her, & belittle her but failed. U would think she was unbreakable bcuz of how resilient she is. When U sum her up, she is simply the Greatest Fighter of all time. ~TR.

MISS TOUGH ONE

Some Ppl may think they know all about U, but they don't. Ppl think they could walk a mile in your footwear, but they can't. Ppl need to mind their own business, but they won't. Some ppl will stress U out & they don't care. There are 2 types of ppl in the world. Hammers & Nails. Something is telling me you're a hammer, bcuz your strength from within hits hard when the struggle is real. ~TR

PSA

Females are Emotionally driven, crazy to a limit (lol), thoughtful to know end & supportive from the heart. They are the foundation to the house, the backbone of everything, & the key to the future. Men will never truly figure out how women are wired (lol). Just Respect what they say, listen to her vent, lend a shoulder when she needs one, & try to never make her feel insecure~TR

SHE'S A MIRACLE

They call her grandma (nana), mom dukes (mommy/mum), sister (sibling), wife (better half), daughter (baby), & friend (bff). She goes by many names, she wears many hats, & she does many jobs. Her heart is out in the open even when she tries to hide it. Her emotions are always running hard, & her hopes are aiming high. She is optimistic, dreams big, goes after her goals, & will do her best to accomplish them. She inspires ppl with her drive, makes ppl happy with her smile, & her kindness makes her genuine/humble. ~TR

HER GUIDELINES

She values herself by setting boundaries that she respects & won't cross. Her time is precious, her attention is meaningful, & she's not about wasting it on BS. She wants to spend her energy on positive things. She wants to be happy more than sad. She wants to be spoken to with respect. She is a lady that will always give but when she gives, she hopes that it's appreciated. If U knew what it took for her to get to where she is now, U could only applaud her. She never took good ppl for granted, for she knows what good ppl mean to her. For that she will always be a blessing to others. ~TR

SHE IS AWESOME

Always believe in yourself & have faith in your abilities to do great things. Not sure if U know this, but U have the ability to change someone's life just by the way U communicate with them. This super power of yours should never go to waste, bcuz picking others up will always be needed in this world. ~TR

IT'S NEVER OVER

If U knew the anxiety that she deals with, U might not be able to handle it. The pool of depression she swims in from time to time, U would probably drown. When she's at the end of her rope & ready to just give up on herself, U have no clue of her struggle. Idk a lot about everything, but what I do know is that, she is something special. Bcuz of her wounded heart, the way she hides the pain, the way she cry's alone, & the way she keeps it together after being broken into pieces. U can't imagine how amazingly tough her soul must be~TR

ABOUT THE AUTHOR

Tony Rogers grew up as one of five children, raised by a hard-working single mother in Newark, New Jersey who taught him to see the grit along with the good in this world.

After earning his BA in Communications from St. Francis College in Brooklyn, NY, Tony ventured North to the Capital District where he pursued a rewarding career working with youth both in and out of the classroom. He describes it as "One of the most influential times of my life and I thoroughly enjoyed every second of it".

Tony Rogers is a man on a mission. "Ever since childhood, I've focused on seeing the positive in every situation and spreading empowerment to others." This perspective served Tony well in life, which in his spare time, he began spreading daily motivational messages to his friends and followers where the idea for a book was born. "Sometimes, all it takes is a small gesture or kind word to help people feel good about themselves. That's all I'm hoping to do." And Tony Rogers does it well.

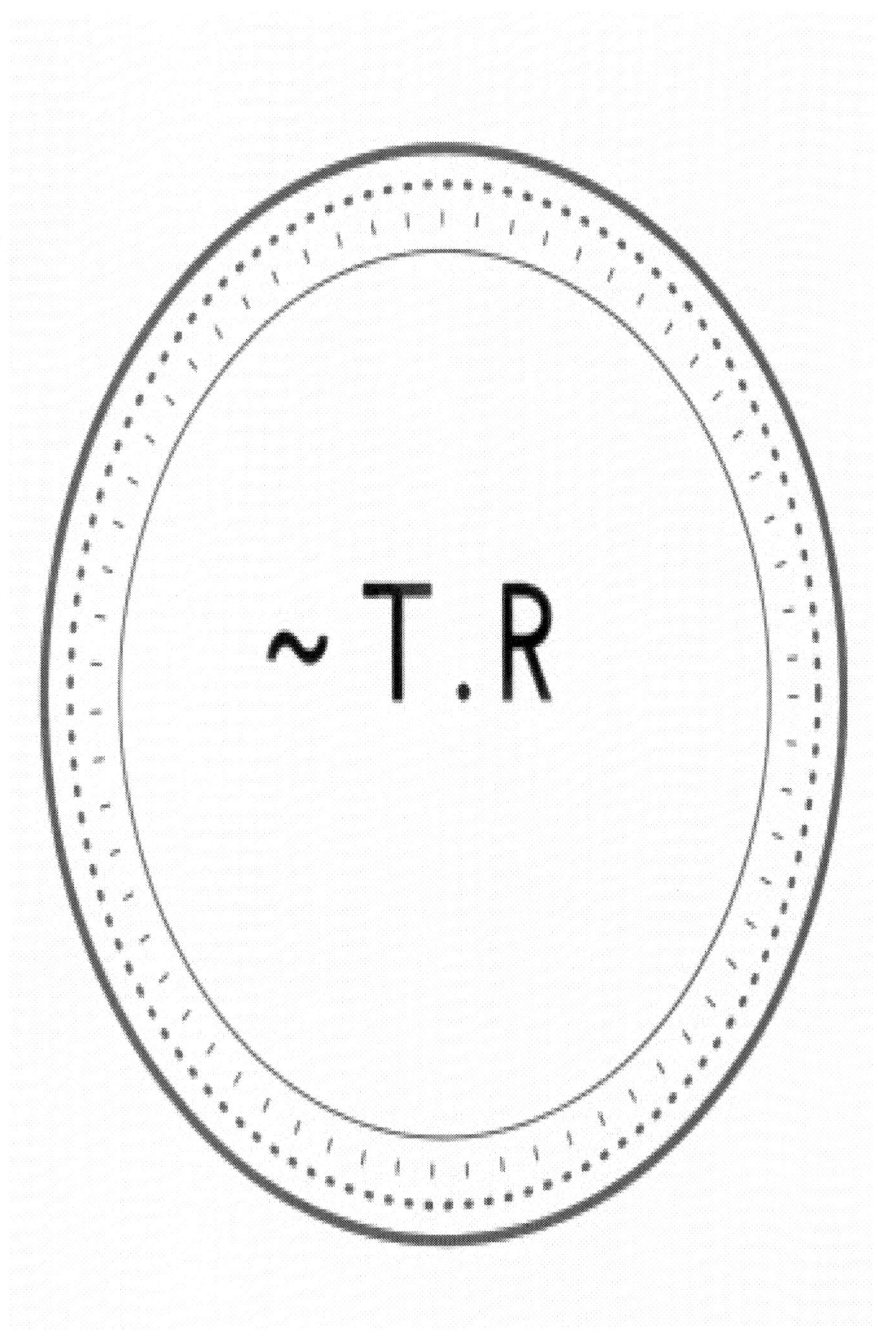
~T.R

Made in the USA
Middletown, DE
24 August 2024

59094896R00035